Library of Congress Cataloging-in-Publication Data
Rundgren, Helen, 1956–
[Världens bästa näsa. English]
The world's best noses, ears, and eyes / by Helen Rundgren and Ingela P. Arrhenius ; translated by Helle Martens. — First American edition.
pages cm
Audience: Age 6–10.
Audience: Grade 4 to 6.
First published in Sweden as: Världens bästa näsa / Helen Rundgren, Ingela P. Arrhenius. Stockholm : Alfabeta, 2013.
ISBN 978-0-8234-3161-8 (hardcover)
1. Animals—Sense organs—Juvenile literature. 2. Animals—Physiology—Juvenile literature. I. Arrhenius, Ingela P., 1967– illustrator. II. Title.
QL945.R8613 2014
591.4—dc23
2013044763

The World's Best

By **Helen Rundgren**

Illustrated by **Ingela P. Arrhenius**

Noses,

Ears,
and Eyes

Holiday House / New York

Ears are for hearing,
eyes are for seeing,
and **noses** collect smells.

But what is there to see? What are we trying to hear?

And pee-ew! What is that smell?

Noses!

Many animals think their nose is the best in the world. Animal noses can be very different from human noses. They can smell all sorts of scents that we can't, and some animal noses can pick up unusual smells that no other animals can. Noses can be long, short, beautiful, or funny looking. But which one is the best? That depends!

HEDGEHOG

If you are out and about at nighttime, you must either be able to see well in the dark or be good at detecting odors. You need to be able to sniff out pancakes, bugs, and other tasty-smelling things. From my hiding place, I can smell delicious food being made at your house.

I have the world's best nose for smelling pancakes!

MOTH

No, I have the best nose in the world. It's true!
It isn't an ordinary, middle-of-the-face nose—it's much better.
I have a double nose. It's pretty, and it can detect
teeny, tiny smells in the air. Itsy-bitsy smells
that humans could never detect.
I can smell a female moth
a mile away.

My super-smelling antennae noses are the best in the world!

Dog

I read all the latest doggy news when I'm out for a walk. You probably can't tell who just passed by, when they were there, or how they were feeling. But I know everything there is to know about the dogs, cats, humans, and garbage cans in my neighborhood.

ELEPHANT

A nose? What exactly do you mean by nose? I have the world's best trunk. It's a multipurpose nose! It's so strong I can lift a tree with it. I can use the tip as a finger and pick out tasty morsels for lunch. I can use my trunk to suck up water and spray it on myself—or, *tee-hee*, on others!

Arm, crane, finger, or shower, my super, multipurpose nose is the best!

POLAR BEAR

I live in vast, wide-open spaces. Standing on my tippy-toes on top of a small iceberg, I lift my nose to sniff the air. I can smell my dinner—the scent of a seal—from a half mile away. Beat that!

I have the world's most amazing long-distance-smelling nose.

SEAL

My nose is the best because I can close it up.

Closed!

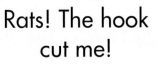

SHARK

Smell or taste, what difference does it make? Although I can't smell much of anything in the air, I can taste tiny traces of smells underwater. Humans use smell and taste together too, but they can't do it underwater. I have the world's best underwater nose because I can detect just a few drops of blood in the sea.

No drop of blood is too small for me!

STAR-NOSED MOLE

You can tell just from my name that I'm fantastic; I dazzle like a star.
That's because my nose is shaped like a star. I smell by wiggling
my twenty-two tentacles.

**I have the world's most amazing
star-shaped nose!**

The human nose is pretty good.
It does the job. But which
of the other animals is right?
Which one has the best nose
in the world?

Ears!

Who has the best ears in the world?
Ears that hear the most? Ears that
can hear from farthest away?
Ears that pick up the slightest sounds?
How do you know if you have the
best ears in the world?
It all depends on who you are and
what sounds you want to hear.

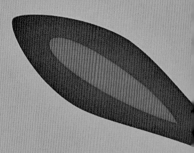

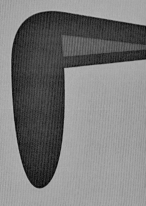

LIZARD

I have the best ears in the world because they don't get in my way. They consist of a hole with an eardrum over it and a few parts inside. That's enough for me to detect everything I need to hear. My ears have no flaps that get caught on bushes. I can hear the vibrations big animals make when they walk, as well as the rustling of small, tasty animals.

I certainly have the best ears in the world.

BAT

I have batty ears. They are the world's best for hearing high-pitched echolocation. You humans can't hear us; our sounds are too high-pitched. When the sounds I make bounce off an insect, a leaf, a door, or a friend, I know its size and shape from the sounds that come back to me. I hear what shapes look like! This is handy, since I only go out at night when it's dark. Can you hear what things look like? No, you can't.

I have the best ears in the world.

ELEPHANT

My ears are the best in the world because they let me hear extremely low, rumbling sounds. Elephants speak a secret language that's too low for humans to hear. We can talk to each other even if we're almost two miles apart! "Hello there!" We don't need cell phones. Also, my ears can shoo away bugs. And my ears tell my mood. If I come galloping and flapping my ears, watch out! That means I'm mad!

I have the biggest and most flappable ears in the world.

RABBIT

My ears are world-class. They are like adjustable satellite dishes. I can move one ear at a time and pick up sounds from different directions. I can lower them so they're hidden. My ears are fantastic. I hear everything! All those sounds make me a little nervous sometimes, but I do have the best ears in the world.

Look at my satellite dish ears!

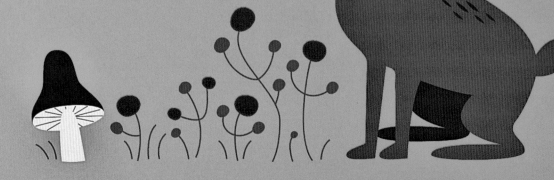

CRICKET

No, my ears are the best, the most unique, and the most beautiful. My ears are not where you would expect to find them—they're under my knees. This is useful when I use my legs to play music. I can hear if I'm on key. With my eyes facing one way and my ears facing another, I'm all set. You should try it too!

Sounds good!

I have the best ear-legs in the world!

Comparing ears isn't easy. They are all so different. Human ears are all right but not great. We can only hear sounds in the middle ranges, but that is good enough for us. Who would want to hear everything all the time anyway? That would be awful. Our eardrums are good at capturing sounds but not so good for flapping.

Eyes!

Many animals have fantastic eyes, but who has the best eyesight? Are the best eyes the ones that can see the farthest or the ones that can see in the dark? Some animals don't see very much, but they see exactly what they need to see. They have good eyes too. But who has the very best eyes of all?

GIRAFFE

I have the best eyes in the world. They are on a stick. Well, not an ordinary stick but on my long, long neck. From way up here, my magnificent eyes can see great distances. Of all the mammals, I can see the farthest—far across the savanna. My eyes are pretty too. I have great big, brown eyes with long, thick lashes that help me shoo away flies.

Hello up here!

Hello!

I have the world's best elevated eyes!

PEACOCK MANTIS SHRIMP

My eyes are good. Really good. They are the best in the world for seeing in color, at least underwater. I have the finest color-detecting eyes. Red, blue, green, yellow—but that's not all! I see colors humans don't even know about. I can't describe them, but they are beautiful.

I have the world's best color-detecting eyes.

OCTOPUS

I have the best eyes in the world. Naturally, the biggest are the best. Wouldn't you agree if you had eyes the size of big dinner plates? See, these are what I call eyes. They are excellent for identifying what I'm eating—even in the deepest, darkest spots at the bottom of the ocean.

The best eyes in the world are the biggest ones, and they belong to me.

BIRDS OF PREY

Flying high above, we can see tiny animals on the ground and fish swimming in the water. Although we scout for different types of food, we birds of prey are all excellent fliers, soaring and scouting. Our eyes are by far the best. We see the slightest movements from high above.
Wheee, here comes a dive!

Birds of prey have the best dinner-scouting eyes.

CAT

I have the best eyes in the world because I am a cat, and cats have the best eyes in the world. We have slit pupils and special reflectors at the backs of our eyes that give us excellent night vision.

I have the world's best night-vision eyes.

SNAIL

But I think my eyes are the best because I can see around corners. Everyone should have eyes on stalks.

FLY

The best eyes in the world are made up of many small eyes that can look in different directions all at once. Backward, forward, this way, that way. Nothing can sneak up on me. I notice the slightest movement anywhere. Why have two eyes when you can have compound eyes? Now that's smart!!

I have the world's best compound eyes.

It's hard to decide which would be better: compound eyes, big eyes, or eyes on stalks. If we compare them to others, human eyes are only average. We can see fairly well, but we can't look behind ourselves. We can't see very much in the dark. Our eyes are not the fastest. They are all right but definitely not the best.

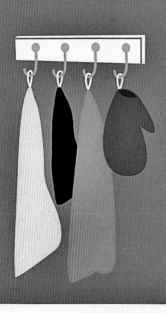

We humans are pretty average. We see just what we need to see, hear just what we need to hear, and can smell well enough to get by. So what do we do best?